Baby's First Quilts

NANCY J. MARTIN

Martingale®
& COMPANY

Dedication

Dedicated to Megan Jane Martin, my granddaughter, who inspired me to make my first special baby quilt 12 years ago.

Acknowledgments

Many thanks to:

The fine quilters who helped me finish the quilts on time: Sarah Borntrager, Susie Hostetler, Jacque Noard, Shelly Nolte, Frankie Schmitt, and Freda Smith.

Cleo Nollette, who made the perfect cover quilt with matching label.

The Martingale & Company staff who always produce a quality book.

Baby's First Quilts
© 2008 by Nancy J. Martin

That Patchwork Place® is an imprint of Martingale & Company®.

Martingale & Company
20205 144th Ave. NE
Woodinville, WA 98072-8478 USA
www.martingale-pub.com

Credits

President & CEO ~ Tom Wierzbicki
Publisher ~ Jane Hamada
Editorial Director ~ Mary V. Green
Managing Editor ~ Tina Cook
Technical Editor ~ Laurie Baker
Copy Editor ~ Marcy Heffernan
Design Director ~ Stan Green
Production Manager ~ Regina Girard
Illustrator ~ Adrienne Smitke
Cover & Text Designer ~ Stan Green
Photographer ~ Brent Kane

Printed in China
13 12 11 10 09 08   8 7 6 5 4 3 2 1

Library of Congress Cataloging-in-Publication Data
Library of Congress Control Number: 2008031665

ISBN: 978-1-56477-744-7

Mission Statement

Dedicated to providing quality products and service to inspire creativity.

Contents

Projects

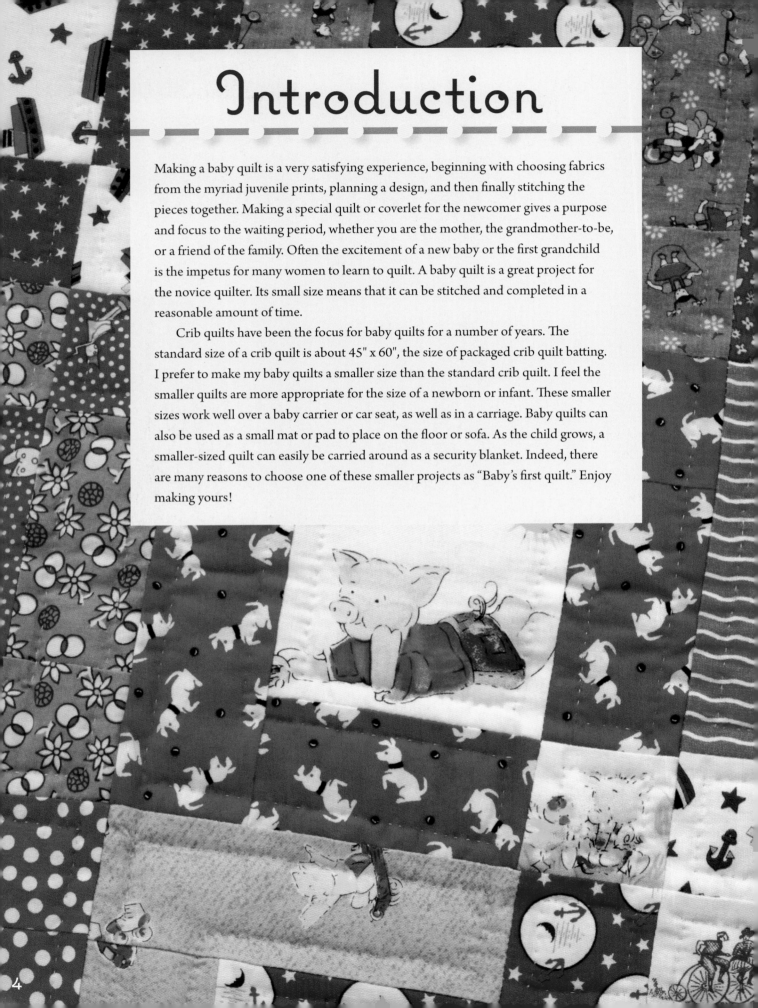

Introduction

Making a baby quilt is a very satisfying experience, beginning with choosing fabrics from the myriad juvenile prints, planning a design, and then finally stitching the pieces together. Making a special quilt or coverlet for the newcomer gives a purpose and focus to the waiting period, whether you are the mother, the grandmother-to-be, or a friend of the family. Often the excitement of a new baby or the first grandchild is the impetus for many women to learn to quilt. A baby quilt is a great project for the novice quilter. Its small size means that it can be stitched and completed in a reasonable amount of time.

Crib quilts have been the focus for baby quilts for a number of years. The standard size of a crib quilt is about 45" x 60", the size of packaged crib quilt batting. I prefer to make my baby quilts a smaller size than the standard crib quilt. I feel the smaller quilts are more appropriate for the size of a newborn or infant. These smaller sizes work well over a baby carrier or car seat, as well as in a carriage. Baby quilts can also be used as a small mat or pad to place on the floor or sofa. As the child grows, a smaller-sized quilt can easily be carried around as a security blanket. Indeed, there are many reasons to choose one of these smaller projects as "Baby's first quilt." Enjoy making yours!

Choosing Fabrics

One of the most enjoyable parts of making a baby quilt is choosing the fabrics. With the many novelty and juvenile prints available, you may be tempted to make two or three of these small wonders. Fabric manufacturers are now producing juvenile novelty prints that feature paper dolls, cowboys, children's toys, nursery rhymes, adventure themes, and cartoon characters. Because the scale of these fabrics is quite large, they are best used for the largest pieces of the block so that you can see the whole design. If you cut the novelty fabric into small pieces, you lose the context of the fabric.

A simple setting that frames the design works well with a novelty print. This focuses the attention on the detail of the design. To find a common size that will work for most of the designs on the fabric, make an expandable window from two L-shaped cardboard pieces. Place this window on the different elements in the fabric, noting the size needed to accommodate each design. Look for a common size that will work for most of the designs; unfortunately, not all the motifs may be the same size. Once you determine a common size, add ¼"-wide seam allowances on all sides and cut the necessary pieces. The fabric motifs may not be evenly spaced, and you may need to skip around the fabric, rather than cut in even rows. This technique is commonly known as "fussy cutting."

Fussy cutting takes a little more time, but the result is well worth the effort because it shows the novelty prints to their best advantage.

The fabric requirements given in this book are generous and based on yardage that is 42" wide after prewashing. If your fabric is wider than 42", there will be a little left over at the end of your strips. If your fabric is narrower than 42", you may need to cut an extra strip to get the required number of pieces. Save any extra yardage for future scrap quilts.

Many of the yardage amounts in this book specify fat quarters. A fat quarter is an 18" x 21" piece of fabric rather than the standard quarter yard that is cut selvage to selvage and measures 9" x 42". Another common size is the fat eighth, which measures 9" x 21". Look for fat quarters and fat eighths that have been cut and bundled at your local quilt shop.

Personalizing Your Quilt

Color is one of the most important design elements of a quilt, so don't limit your color options to the color choices that are pictured here. In fact, color is the easiest change to make to personalize a quilt.

Although I enjoy making scrap quilts with many fabrics, it's much faster and easier to select only three or four fabrics for your quilt. You will have less fabric to handle and cut, and fewer color-value decisions to make as you stitch.

To select fabrics for your quilt, first look to see if the quilt has a background on which the pattern will appear. Most quilts do. If so, select your background first. Don't limit your choices just to solid colors, because they will emphasize mismatched seams and irregular quilting stitches. If you are a beginner who is sill perfecting your piecing and quilting skills, select a print for your background that will help hide minor imperfections. A background print that is nondirectional and still appears unified after being cut apart and resewn is a good choice. Prints with a white background have a clean formal look; those with a beige or tan background resemble prints used in antique quilts and will have a more informal look.

"Tippy Triangles" (page 25) is a great design to use with novelty prints because it easily accommodates 6" finished squares (cut size: 6½" x 6½"), which is a size that I often find in novelty prints. My initial way of using this design was to focus on the bold black-and-white prints and accent them with red, especially since black-and-white images are those that a baby first sees. Later I was drawn to a delightful print called "Duck, Duck, Goose" which also featured 6" squares. Notice the difference in the two color combinations and the different border treatments. Often juvenile or novelty prints have a border design printed along one selvage edge. If you buy a yard of the novelty print for the blocks, there will not be enough of the border design to make a complete border around the quilt. Notice

that in both quilts, the border was cut into pieces and stitched to other fabrics to make a pieced border.

Tippy Triangles

Duck Duck Goose

When the size of the novelty print is larger than 6", or is quite busy, it is best to use a simple pattern such as "Framed Square" (page 28). The colorful dolls in native costume are quite detailed in this delightful baby-girl quilt. In the alternate version, I framed bright 10" square handkerchiefs printed with nursery-rhyme themes.

"This and That" (page 32) is a design that frames rectangular pieces of a novelty print, a shape which shows the fabric motifs to their best advantage. If your fabric motif happens to be square, it is easy to adapt the design to a square shape as I did for "Childhood Daze".

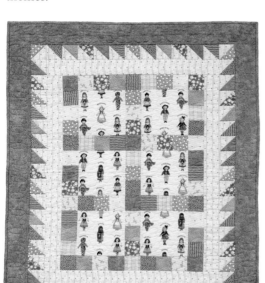

Framed Square

This and That

Nursery Rhyme

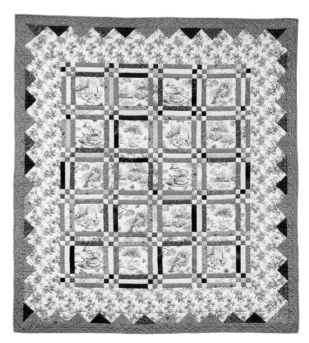

Childhood Daze

The obvious quilt color variation can simply be blue for boys and pink for girls, traditional but effective. This color change was my first variation in "Nana's First Quilt" (page 38). To add to that variation, the blue quilt has an inner border before the outer border of plaid squares, while the pink quilt has an inner border of plaid squares and an outer border of pink plaid fabric. Don't hesitate to make simple variations such as this to your quilt.

Novelty prints can serve many uses in a quilt design. Though frequently used as a focal point in the largest square of each block, novelty prints can also make an effective border, as shown in the yellow-and-blue version of "Paper Dolls" (page 54). The same design, using a different coloration of the novelty print, changes to a softer focus when sewn in light and dark green print fabrics.

Nana's First Quilt (blue)

Paper Dolls (blue)

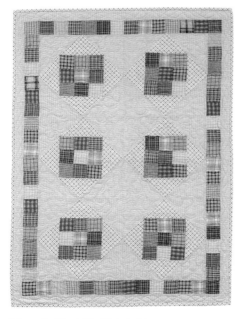

Nana's First Quilt (pink)

Paper Dolls (green)

Tools of the Trade

Quiltmaking requires some basic tools. The following is a list of items I use each time I make a project:

Rotary cutter and mat: A large rotary cutter enables you to quickly cut strips and pieces without templates. A cutting mat is essential to protect both the blade and the table on which you're cutting. An 18" x 24" mat allows you to cut long strips, on the straight or bias grain. You might also consider purchasing a smaller mat to use when working with scraps.

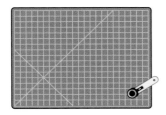

Rotary-cutting rulers: Use a see-through ruler to measure and guide the rotary cutter. There are many appropriate rulers on the market. Make sure the one you choose includes marks for 45° and 60° angles and guidelines for cutting strips in standard-sized measurements. Select a ruler that is marked with large, clear numbers and does not have a lot of confusing lines.

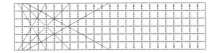

The Bias Square® ruler is critical for cutting accurate bias squares. This acrylic ruler is available in three sizes, 4", 6", or 8" square, and is ruled with ⅛" marks. It features a diagonal line, which is placed on the bias seam, enabling you to cut an accurately sewn square that looks as if it were made from two triangles.

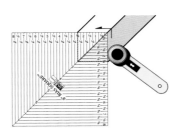

Sewing machine: Stitching quilts on a sewing machine is easy and enjoyable. Spend some time getting to know your machine and becoming comfortable using it. Keep your machine dust free and well oiled.

Machine piecing does not require an elaborate sewing machine. All you need is a straight-stitch machine in good working order. It should make an evenly locked straight stitch that looks the same on both sides of the stitching. Adjust the tension, if necessary, to produce smooth, even seams. A puckered seam causes the fabric to curve, distorting the size and shape of the piecing and the quilt you're making.

Pins: A good supply of glass- or plastic-headed pins is necessary. Long pins are especially helpful when pinning thick layers together. If you plan to machine quilt, you will need to hold the layers of the quilt together with a large supply of rustproof, size 2 safety pins.

Iron and ironing board: Frequent and careful pressing is necessary to ensure a smooth, accurately stitched quilt top. Place your iron and ironing board, along with a plastic spray bottle of water, close to your sewing machine.

Needles: Use sewing-machine needles sized for cotton fabrics (size 70/10 or 80/12). You also need hand-sewing needles (Sharps) and hand-quilting needles (Betweens #8, #9, and #10).

Scissors: Use good-quality shears, and use them only for cutting fabric. Thread snips or embroidery scissors are handy for clipping stray threads.

Seam ripper: This little tool will come in handy if you find it necessary to remove a seam before resewing.

Quiltmaking Basics

In this section, you'll find instructions for the techniques used throughout this book to make the quilt tops and to finish your quilts.

Basic Bias-Square Technique

Many traditional quilt patterns contain squares made from two contrasting half-square triangles. The short sides of the triangles are on the straight grain of fabric while the long sides are on the bias. These are called bias-square units. Using a bias strip-piecing method, you can easily sew and cut large amounts of bias squares. This technique is especially useful for small bias squares, as pressing after stitching usually distorts the shape (and sometimes results in burned fingers).

Note: *All instructions in this book give the cut size for bias squares; the finished size after stitching will be ½" smaller.*

To make bias squares:

1. Start with two squares of fabric. The instructions in this book call for a pair of 8" x 8" or 9" x 9" squares. Layer the squares right sides up and cut in half diagonally.

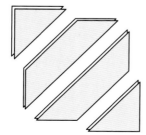

2. Cut the squares into strips the width indicated in the instructions, measuring from the previous cut.

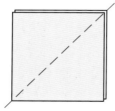

3. Arrange and stitch alternate pieces from each square together using ¼"-wide seam allowances. Be sure to align the strips so the lower edge and one adjacent edge form straight lines.

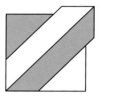

4. Starting at the lower-left corner, align the 45° mark of the Bias Square ruler on the seam line. Each bias square will require two cuts. The first cut is along the side and the top edge. It removes the bias square from the rest of the fabric and is made slightly larger than the correct size, as shown in the series of illustrations below.

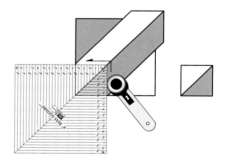

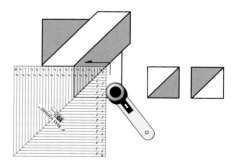

Align 45° mark on seam line
and cut first 2 sides.

5. The second cut is made along the remaining two sides. It aligns the diagonal and trims the bias square to the correct size. To make the cut, turn the segment and place the Bias Square on the opposite two sides, aligning the required measurements on both sides of the cutting guide and the 45° mark on the seam. Cut the remaining two sides of the bias squares.

Turn cut segments and cut opposite 2 sides.

6. Continue cutting bias squares from each unit in this manner, working from left to right and from bottom to top, row by row, until you have cut bias squares from all usable fabric.

If you are designing your own quilts or changing the size of the blocks used in the project instructions, use the chart below to determine strip width and how many bias squares you can expect to cut from two squares of fabric.

Finished Size	Cut Size	Fabric Size	Strip Width	Yield
1½"	2" x 2"	7" x 7"	2"	8
2"	2½" x 2½"	8" x 8"*	2½"	8
2"	2½" x 2½"	9" x 9"	2½"	14
2⅛"	2⅝" x 2⅝"	8" x 8"	2½"	8
2½"	3" x 3"	8" x 8"	2¾"	8
2½"	3" x 3"	9" x 9"	2¾"	8
3"	3½" x 3½"	9" x 9"	3"	8
A pair of 7" x 7" squares will yield the same number of bias squares.				

Machine Piecing

It's important to be comfortable with the sewing machine you're using. If this is your first machine-made quilt, practice guiding fabric through the machine. If you leave the machine unthreaded, you can practice over and over on the same pieces of fabric.

Operating a sewing machine requires the same type of coordination it takes to drive a car. Use your foot to control the machine's speed and your hands to control the fabric's direction. To start, use your right foot for the foot pedal to manage the speed. If the machine goes too fast at first, slip a sponge under a hinge-type pedal to slow it down. Use your hands to guide the fabric that feeds into the machine.

A good habit to develop is to use a seam ripper or long pin to gently guide the fabric up to the needle. You can hold seam intersections together or make minor adjustments before the fabric is sewn.

The most important skill in machine piecing is sewing an accurate ¼"-wide seam allowance. This is necessary for seams to match and for the resulting block or quilt to measure the required size. There are several methods that will help you achieve this.

- Purchase a special foot that is sized so that you can align the edge of your fabric with the edge of the presser foot, resulting in a seam that is ¼" from the fabric edge. Bernina has a special patchwork foot (#37) and Little Foot makes several special ¼" feet that fit most machines.

- If you have an electronic or computerized sewing machine, adjust the needle position so that the resulting seam is ¼" from the fabric edge.

- Find the ¼" seam allowance on your machine by placing an accurate template under the presser foot and lowering the needle onto the seam line; mark the seam allowance by placing a piece of masking tape at the edge of the template. You can use several layers of masking tape, building up a raised edge to guide your fabric. You can also use a piece of moleskin for a raised seam guide.

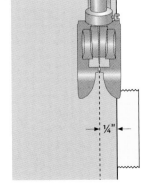

Test to make sure that the method you're using results in an accurate ¼"-wide seam allowance.

1. Cut three strips of fabric, 1½" x 3".

2. Sew the strips together using the edge of the presser foot or the seam guide you have made.

3. Press the seam allowances toward the outer edges. After sewing and pressing, the center strip should measure exactly 1" wide. If it doesn't, adjust the needle or seam guide in the proper direction.

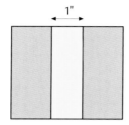

MATCHING SEAMS

When sewing the fabric pieces that make up a unit or block, follow the piecing diagram provided. Press each group of pieces before joining it to the next unit.

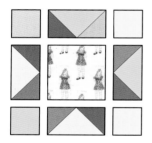
Stitch, then press.

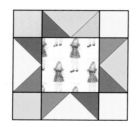
Join units together.

There are several techniques you can use to get your seams to match perfectly.

Opposing seam allowances: When stitching one seamed unit to another, press seam allowances of pieces to be joined in opposite directions. The two "opposing" seam allowances will hold each other in place and evenly distribute the fabric bulk. Plan pressing to take advantage of opposing seam allowances.

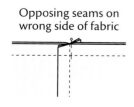
Opposing seams on wrong side of fabric | Accurate match on right side of fabric

Positioning pin: A pin, carefully pushed straight through two points that need to match and pulled tight, will establish the proper matching point. Pin the remainder of the seam normally and remove the positioning pin just before stitching.

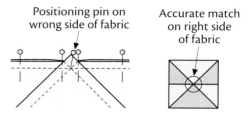
Positioning pin on wrong side of fabric | Accurate match on right side of fabric

The X: When triangles are pieced, the stitches will form an X at the next seam line. Stitch through the center of the X to make sure the points on the sewn triangles will not be cut off.

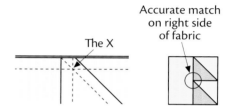
The X | Accurate match on right side of fabric

Easing: When two pieces you're sewing together are supposed to match but are slightly different in length, pin the points to match and stitch with the shorter piece on top. The feed dogs will ease the fullness of the bottom piece.

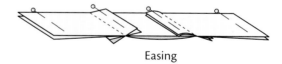
Easing

Inspect each intersection from the right side to see that it is matched. If the seams don't meet accurately, note which direction the fabric needs to be moved. Use a seam ripper to rip out the seam intersection and ½" of stitching on either side of the intersection. Shift fabric to correct the alignment, place positioning pins, and then restitch.

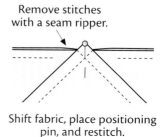
Remove stitches with a seam ripper.

Shift fabric, place positioning pin, and restitch.

Pressing: After stitching a seam, it is important to press your work. Careful pressing helps make the next steps in the stitching process, such as matching points or aligning seams, easier.

Be sure to press, not iron, your work. Ironing is an aggressive back-and-forth motion that we use on clothing to remove wrinkles. This action can easily pull and distort the bias edges or seams in your piecing. Perfectly marked and sewn quilt pieces are commonly distorted by excessive ironing.

MATCHING BLOCKS

After you make the required number of blocks, assemble them into rows. The blocks in each row should be pinned together at strategic intersections to ensure accurate matching as rows are sewn together. The process is similar to matching seams within a block.

To make this process easier, plan for opposing seam allowances when you press blocks after stitching. Press seam allowances in opposite directions from row to row.

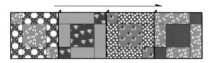

Row 1 — Press seams to right.

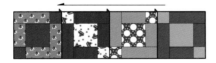

Row 2 — Press seams to left.

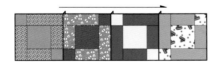

Row 3 — Press seams to right.

If the blocks have points, such as the "Tippy Triangles" block shown, the points of adjoining blocks should meet ¼" from the raw edge.

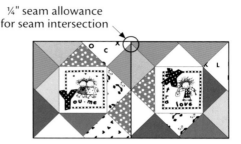

¼" seam allowance for seam intersection

Use positioning pins to hold seam allowances in place. Remove the pins before stitching through the seam intersection.

Positioning pin

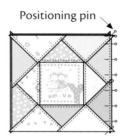

CHAIN PIECING

Chain piecing is an assembly-line approach to putting your blocks together. Rather than sewing each block from start to finish, you can sew identical units of each block together at one time, streamlining the process. It's a good idea, however, to sew one sample block together from start to finish to ensure that the pieces have been accurately cut and that you have the proper positioning and coloration for each piece.

1. Stack the units you will be sewing in pairs, arranging any opposing seam allowances so that the seam allowance on the top unit is pressed toward the needle and the seam allowance on the bottom unit is pressed toward you. Then you won't need to keep checking to see if the lower seam is being

pulled to the wrong side by the feed dogs as you feed the fabric through the sewing machine.

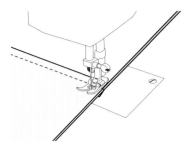

Face top seam allowance toward the needle whenever possible.

2. Feed units through the machine without stopping to cut thread. There will be a "stitch" or small length of thread between the units.

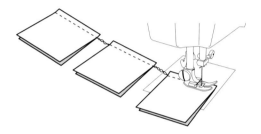

3. Take the connected units to the ironing board for pressing, and then clip them apart. Chain piecing takes a little planning, but it saves you time and thread.

Helpful Hint

Keep a stack of fabric scraps, about 2" x 2", near your machine. When you begin to sew, fold one of the squares in half and sew to its edge. This folded piece of fabric is called a thread saver. Leave the presser foot down and continue sewing onto your piecing unit. When you have finished sewing a seam or chain piecing, sew onto another thread saver, leaving the needle in place and the presser foot down. This thread saver will be in place for sewing the next seam or unit.

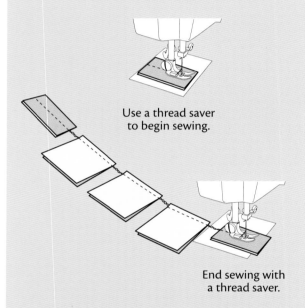

Use a thread saver to begin sewing.

End sewing with a thread saver.

This technique saves thread because you don't stop and pull a length of thread to remove fabric from the machine. All the tails of thread will be on the thread saver and not on the back of the block or quilt. This method also keeps the machine from eating the edges of the fabric as you start a seam.

Finishing Techniques

This section includes tips for completing a quilt with confidence and pride. What I suggest works well for me, but is by no means the only way to accomplish the job. If a technique is new to you, try it; you might find that you incorporate the technique into your quiltmaking process from now on.

Adding Borders

Borders can be used to frame and soften a busy design. It isn't always necessary to have a border on a quilt, however. Many antique quilts made from scraps have no borders because continuous yardage was scarce and expensive.

Straighten the edges of your quilt top before adding borders. There should be little or no trimming needed for a straight-set quilt.

All of the projects in this book have borders with butted corners. The measurements given in the cutting instructions for the border strips are longer than necessary to allow for any variances in the quilt-top size. Trim them to the exact size before adding them to the quilt top. To find the correct measurement for butted border strips, always measure through the center of the quilt, not at the outside edges. This ensures that the borders are of equal length on opposite sides of the quilt and brings the outer edges in line with the center dimension if discrepancies exist. Otherwise, your quilt might not be "square" due to minor piecing variations and/or stretching that occurred while you worked with the pieces. If there is a large size difference between the two sides, it is better to go back and correct the source of the problem rather than try to make the border fit and end up with a distorted quilt.

You will save fabric if you attach the border strips to the longest sides first, and then stitch the border strips to the remaining two sides.

1. Measure the length of the quilt through the center. Trim two border strips to this measurement.

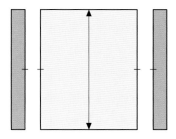

Measure center of quilt, top to bottom.

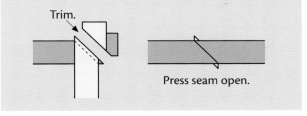

> ## Tip
>
> When joining border strips, the seam will be less noticeable and stronger if it is pieced on an angle. You may need additional fabric to do so.
>
> Trim.
>
> Press seam open.

2. Mark the centers of the border strips and the quilt top. Pin the borders to the sides of the quilt, matching centers and ends and easing or slightly stretching the quilt to fit the border strip as necessary.

3. Sew the side borders in place and press the seam allowances toward the borders.

4. Measure the width of the quilt through the center, including the side borders, to determine the length of the top and bottom borders. Cut the border strips to this measurement, piecing strips as necessary. Mark the centers of the border strips and

the quilt top. Pin borders to the top and bottom of the quilt top, easing or slightly stretching the quilt to fit as necessary.

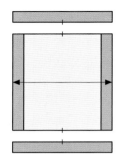

Measure center of quilt,
side to side, including borders.
Mark centers.

5. Sew the top and bottom borders in place and press the seam allowances toward the borders.

Marking the Quilting Design

Whether you machine or hand quilt, you'll need to mark a quilting design on the quilt top. The exceptions are when you're stitching in the ditch, outlining the design ¼" away from all seams, stitching a grid of straight lines using masking tape as a guide, or stitching a meandering, free-motion design.

Stitching in the ditch. To stitch in the ditch, place the stitches in the valley created next to the seam. Stitch on the side that does not have the seam allowance under it.

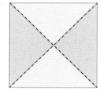

Quilting in the ditch

Outlining. To outline a design, stitch ¼" from seam inside each shape.

Outline quilting

Marking a grid. To mark a grid or pattern of lines, use ¼"-wide masking tape in 15" to 18" lengths. Place strips of tape on a small area and quilt next to the edge of the tape. Remove the tape when stitching is complete. You can reuse the tape to mark another area. Caution: Don't leave tape on a quilt top for an extended length of time, as it may leave a sticky residue.

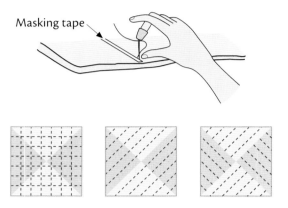

Masking tape

Marking complex designs. To mark complex designs, use a stencil. Quilting stencils made from durable plastic are available in quilt shops. Use stencils to mark repeated designs. There is a groove cut into the plastic, wide enough to allow the use of a marking device. Just place the marker inside the groove to quickly transfer the design to the fabric. Good removable marking pencils include Berol silver pencils, EZ Washout marking pencils, mechanical pencils, and sharp regular pencils. Just be sure to draw lines lightly. Always test any marking device on a scrap of fabric for removability.

Use a light table to trace more intricate designs from books.

To make your own light table:

Separate your dining-room table as if you're adding an extra leaf. Then place a piece of glass, plastic, or Plexiglas over the opening. (I use the removable glass from a storm door for safety's sake, because there is a frame around the edge of the glass.) Have the glass (or glass substitute) cut to fit your table at a glass shop, if desired, and frame or tape the edges to avoid cut fingers. For an additional fee, you can have glass edges finished to eliminate the sharp edges.

Once the glass is in place, position a table lamp on the floor beneath it to create an instant light table. If your table does not separate, two card tables or end tables of the same height can be pushed together to create a support for the glass.

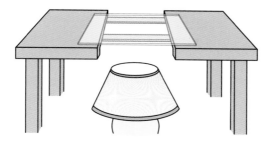

Backing

Because these quilts are small, you will be able to use one length of fabric for all of the quilts but "Beach Balls" (page 57). For that quilt, you will need to seam two lengths of fabric together to achieve the correct size. Cut your backing 3" to 4" larger than the quilt top all around. Avoid the temptation to use a bed sheet for a backing, as it is difficult to quilt through.

Batting

There are many types of batting to choose from, but lightweight battings are best for baby quilts. A lightweight batting is easier to quilt through and shows the quilting design well. It also gives your quilt an antique, old-fashioned look. Polyester batting works well, doesn't shift after washing, and is easy to quilt through. Cotton batting is a good choice if you want to achieve the look of a vintage quilt. This batting must be quilted with stitches no more than 2" apart.

Dark batting works well behind a dark quilt top. If there is any bearding (batting fibers creeping through the top), it will not be as noticeable.

Layering and Basting

Open a package of batting and smooth it out flat. Allow the batting to rest in this position for at least 24 hours. Press the backing so the fold lines have been removed.

A large dining-room table, Ping-Pong table, or two large folding tables pushed together make an ideal work surface on which to prepare your quilt. Use a table pad

to protect your dining-room table. The floor is not a good choice for layering your quilt. It requires you to do too much bending, and the layers can easily shift or be disturbed.

1. Place the backing on the table with the wrong side of the fabric facing up. If the table is large enough, you may want to tape the backing down with masking tape. Spread your batting over the backing, center it, and smooth out any remaining folds.

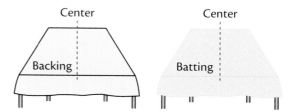

2. Center the freshly pressed and marked quilt top on these two layers. Check all four sides to make sure there is adequate batting and backing. Stretch the backing to make sure it is still smooth.

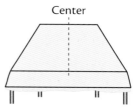

The basting method you use depends on whether you will quilt by hand or machine. Thread basting is used for hand quilting, while safety pin basting is generally used for machine quilting.

THREAD BASTING

1. Starting in the center of the quilt top, baste the three layers together with straight pins while gently smoothing out the fullness to the sides and corners. Take care not to distort the borders and any straight lines within the quilt design.

2. After pinning, baste the layers together with a needle and light-colored thread, so the thread color won't transfer onto the quilt. Start in the middle and make a line of long stitches to each corner to form a large X.

3. Continue basting in a grid of parallel lines 6" to 8" apart. Finish with a row of basting around the outside edges. Quilts that are to be quilted with a hoop or on your lap will be handled more than those quilted on a frame; therefore, they require more basting. After basting, remove the pins. Now you're ready to quilt.

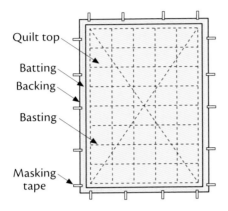

PIN BASTING

A quick way to baste a quilt top is with size 2 safety pins. They are large enough to catch all three layers but not so large that they snag fine fabric. Begin pinning in the center and work out toward the edges. Place pins 4" to 5" apart.

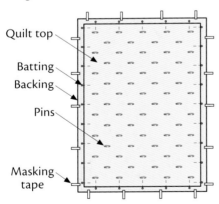

Use long, straight pins along the outside edge to hold everything in place. Place pins perpendicular to the edge, 1½" to 2" apart.

Hand Quilting

To quilt by hand, you need quilting thread, quilting needles, small scissors, a thimble, and perhaps a balloon or large rubber band to help grasp the needle if it gets stuck. Quilt on a frame, a large hoop, on your lap, or a table. Use a single strand of quilting thread not longer than 18". Make a small, single knot at the end of the thread. The quilting stitch is a small running stitch that goes through all three layers of the quilt. Take two, three, or even four stitches at a time if you can keep them even. When crossing seams, you might find it necessary to "hunt and peck" one stitch at a time.

To begin, insert the needle in the top layer about 1" from the point where you want to start stitching. Pull the needle out at the desired starting point and gently tug at the knot until it pops through the fabric and is buried in the batting. Make a backstitch and begin quilting. Stitches should be tiny (8 to 10 per inch is good), even, and straight; tiny stitches will come with practice.

When you come almost to the end of the thread, make a single knot ¼" from the fabric. Take a backstitch to bury the knot in the batting. Run the thread out through the batting and out the quilt top; then snip it off. The first and last stitches will look different from the running stitches in between. To make them less noticeable, start and stop where quilting lines cross each other or at seam joints. Remove the basting when the quilting is finished.

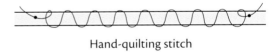

Hand-quilting stitch

Machine Quilting

Machine quilting is a good choice for those who have little time and need to finish their tops in a hurry. It's also a practical choice for baby quilts or other items that will need lots of washing.

Machine quilting works best on small projects; it can be frustrating to feed the bulk of a large quilt through a sewing machine.

Use a walking foot or even-feed foot (or the built-in, even-feed feature on your machine, if available) for your sewing machine to help the quilt layers feed through the machine without shifting or puckering. This type of foot is essential for straight-line and grid quilting and for large, simple curves. Read your machine's instruction manual for special tension settings to sew through extra fabric thicknesses.

Walking foot

Curved designs require free fabric movement under the foot of the sewing machine. This is called free-motion quilting, and with a little practice, you can imitate beautiful hand-quilting designs quickly. If you wish to quilt curved designs with your machine, use a darning foot and lower the feed dogs while using this foot. Because the feed dogs are lowered for free-motion quilting, the speed at which you run the machine and feed the fabric under the foot determines the stitch length. Practice running the machine fairly fast, because this makes it easier to sew smoother lines of quilting. With free-motion quilting, don't turn the fabric under the needle. Instead, guide the fabric as if the needle were a stationary pencil drawing the lines of your design.

Darning foot

Practice first on a piece of fabric until you get the feel of controlling the motion of the fabric with your hands. Stitch some free-form scribbles, zigzags, and curves. Try a heart or a star. Then practice on a sample block with batting and backing. Make sure your chair is adjusted to a comfortable height. This type of quilting may feel awkward at first, but with a little determination and practice you will be able to complete a project with beautiful machine quilting in just a few hours.

Keep the spacing between quilting lines consistent over the entire quilt. Avoid using little, complex designs and leaving large unquilted spaces. For most battings, a 2" or 3" square is the largest area that can be left unquilted. Read the instructions enclosed with the batting you have chosen.

Free-motion meandering pattern

Don't try to machine quilt an entire quilt in one sitting, even if it's a small project. Break the work into short periods, and stretch and relax your muscles regularly.

When all the quilting has been completed, remove the safety pins. Sometimes it is necessary to remove safety pins as you work.

Binding the Edges

My favorite quilt binding is a double-layer French binding made from bias strips. It rolls over the edges of the quilt nicely, and the two layers of fabric resist wear. If you use 2¼"-wide strips, the finished width of this binding will be ⅜".

Double-layer French binding

The quilt instructions tell you how much fabric to purchase for binding. If, however, you enlarge your quilt or need to compute binding fabric, use the following handy chart.

Length of Binding	Fabric Needed
115"	¼ yard*
180"	⅜ yard
255"	½ yard
320"	⅝ yard
400"	¾ yard
465"	⅞ yard

*It's a good idea to purchase ½ yard of fabric instead of ¼ yard so the bias strips will be longer and the binding won't have as many seams.

Determine the distance around your quilt and add about 10" for turning the corners and for overlapping the ends of the binding strips.

After quilting, trim excess batting and backing even with the edge of the quilt top. A rotary cutter and long ruler will ensure accurate straight edges. If the basting is no longer in place, baste all three layers together at the outer edges.

To cut bias strips for binding, follow these steps:

1. Align the 45° angle of a Bias Square along the selvage and place a long ruler's edge against it. Make the first cut.

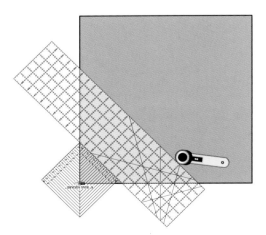

2. Measure the desired width of the strip (2¼") from the cut edge of the fabric. Cut along the edge with the ruler. Continue cutting until you have the number of strips necessary to achieve the required binding length.

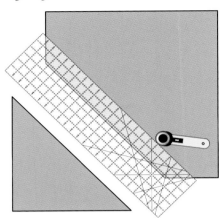

Follow these steps to bind the edges:

1. Stitch the bias strips together, offsetting them as shown, to make one continuous strip. Press the seam allowances open.

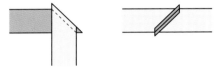

2. Press the strip in half lengthwise, wrong sides together.

3. Unfold the binding at one end and turn the end under ¼" at a 45° angle as shown.

4. Beginning on one side of the quilt, stitch the binding to the quilt using a ¼"-wide seam allowance. Start stitching 1" to 2" from the start of the binding. Stop stitching ¼" from the corner and backstitch.

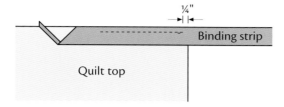

5. Turn the quilt to prepare for sewing along the next edge. Fold the binding away from the quilt as shown, and then fold again to place the binding along the second edge of the quilt. (This fold creates an angled pleat at the corner, called a mitered corner.)

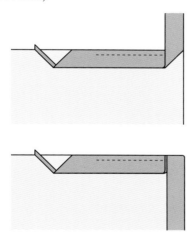

6. Stitch from the fold of the binding along the second edge of the quilt top, stopping ¼" from the corner as you did for the first corner; backstitch. Repeat the stitching and mitering process on the remaining edges and corners of the quilt.

7. When you reach the beginning of the binding, cut the end 1" longer than needed and tuck the end inside the beginning. Stitch the rest of the binding.

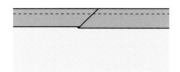

8. Turn the binding to the back of the quilt, over the raw edges, and blindstitch in place so that the folded edge covers the row of machine stitching. At each corner, fold the binding as shown to form a miter on the back of the quilt.

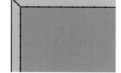

Quilt Labels

It's a good idea to label a quilt with its name, the name and address of the maker, and the date on which it was finished. Include the name of the quilter(s) if the quilt was quilted by a group or someone other than the maker. Baby quilts can be given with an extra touch of love and a sentimental message written on the label.

To easily make a label, use a permanent-ink pen to print or legibly write all this information on a piece of muslin. Press freezer paper to the back of the muslin to stabilize it while you write. Press raw edges to the wrong side of the label. Remove the freezer paper and stitch the label securely to a lower corner on the back of the quilt. You can also do labels in cross-stitch or embroidery.

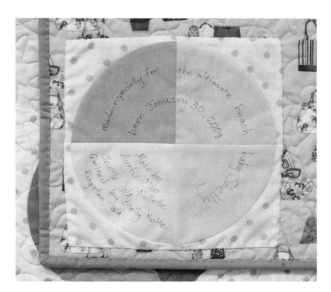

Foursquare

By Nancy J. Martin, Kingston, Washington, 2005.
Quilted by Suzie Hostetler, LaRue, Ohio.

Finished quilt size: 31" x 37"
Finished block size: 6" x 6"

$\mathcal{F}$oursquare is the perfect pattern to showcase juvenile and novelty prints, as well as 1930s reproduction fabrics. With its snappy red-white-and-blue color scheme, this quick and easy project will delight either a baby boy or girl.

Materials

Yardages are based on 42"-wide fabrics.

10 fat eighths of assorted blue fabrics for blocks*

10 fat eighths of assorted red fabrics for blocks*

⅜ yard of blue fabric for outer border

¼ yard of light fabric for inner border

⅜ yard of red fabric for bias binding

1¼ yards of fabric for backing

Batting and thread to finish

Several novelty prints with white backgrounds were included in the red fabric and blue fabric assortments.

Cutting

All measurements include ¼"-wide seam allowances.

From *each* of the 10 fat eighths of assorted red fabrics, cut:
- 1 strip, 2" x 21" (10 total); crosscut into:
  - 2 rectangles, 2" x 5" (20 total)
  - 2 rectangles, 2" x 3½" (20 total)
- 1 square, 3½" x 3½" (10 total)
- 2 squares, 2" x 2" (20 total)

From *each* of the 10 fat eighths of assorted blue fabrics, cut:
- 1 strip, 2" x 21" (10 total); crosscut into:
  - 2 rectangles, 2" x 5" (20 total)
  - 2 rectangles, 2" x 3½" (20 total)
- 1 square, 3½" x 3½" (10 total)
- 2 squares, 2" x 2" (20 total)

From the light fabric, cut:
- 4 strips, 1½" x 42"

From the blue fabric, cut:
- 4 strips, 2¾" x 42"

Making the Blocks

You will make two color combinations of this block, varying the placement of the red and blue prints and occasionally substituting a light background print for the block center and small corner squares. Use pieces cut from the same blue and red fabrics in each block.

1. Stitch a red 2" x 3½" rectangle to the blue 3½" center square.

2. Stitch a blue 2" square to the end of the remaining red 2" x 3½" rectangle to make unit 1. Stitch the remaining blue 2" square to the end of a red 2" x 5" rectangle to make unit 2.

Unit 1   Unit 2

3. Join unit 1 to the bottom of the center square unit.

4. Join the remaining red 2" x 5" rectangle to the left side of the center-square unit, and then add unit 2 to the top.

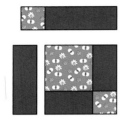
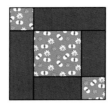

5. Repeat steps 1–4 to make a total of 10 red blocks. Reversing the colors, repeat steps 1–4 to make 10 blue blocks.

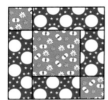
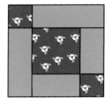

Make 10 of each.

Assembling the Quilt Top

1. Refer to the quilt assembly diagram to arrange and sew the blocks into five rows of four blocks each, alternating the red and blue blocks in each row and from row to row. Join the rows, matching seams.

2. Refer to "Adding Borders" on page 15 to sew the 1½"-wide inner borders to the quilt top. Repeat to add the 2¾"-wide outer borders.

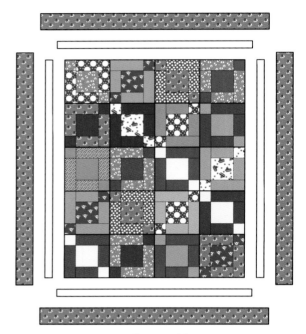

Quilt assembly

Finishing

1. Mark the quilt top with the design of your choice. Layer with batting and backing; baste. Hand or machine quilt as desired.

2. Refer to "Binding the Edges" on page 19 to cut 2¼"-wide bias strips for binding. Make a total of 142" of bias binding and sew it to the quilt.

3. Make a label and attach it to the back of the quilt.

Tippy Triangles

By Nancy J. Martin, Kingston, Washington, 2006.
Quilted by Jacque Noard, Kingston, Washington.

Finished quilt size: 28½" x 40½"
Finished block size: 12" x 12"

Tippy Triangles is a design that can effectively showcase novelty prints. The center portion of the block is cut from 6½" squares. This is such a versatile pattern that I have used it to make dozens of baby quilts.

Materials

Yardages are based on 42"-wide fabrics.

1 yard of black-and-white novelty print for block centers and border*

5 fat eighths of assorted bright red prints for blocks

5 fat eighths of assorted black-and-white prints for blocks and border

⅜ yard of red fabric for bias binding

1¼ yards of fabric for backing

Batting and thread to finish

Depending on the print you select, additional yardage may be needed to fussy cut the block center squares (see page 5).

Cutting

All measurements include ¼"-wide seam allowances. See page 5 for instructions to fussy cut the block center squares from the novelty fabric.

From the black-and-white novelty print, fussy cut:
• 6 squares, 6½" x 6½"

From *each* of the 5 fat eighths of assorted bright red prints, cut:
• 2 squares, 7¼" x 7¼"; cut twice diagonally to yield 8 triangles (40 total; you will have 4 left over)

From *each* of the 5 fat eighths of assorted black-and-white prints, cut:
• 2 squares, 7¼" x 7¼"; cut twice diagonally to yield 8 triangles (40 total; you will have 4 left over)

Making the Blocks

You will make two variations of the same block. Pay careful attention to the placement of the fabrics. Use an assortment of red and black-and-white prints in each block.

1. Sew a red triangle to the top and bottom of three novelty print squares. Stitch a black-and-white print triangle to each side of the squares.

Make 3.

2. Arrange four red triangles and four black-and-white triangles around the center units as shown, noting the color placement. Stitch the triangles at each corner together. Stitch the triangles to the center units, joining opposite sides first.

 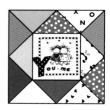

Make 3.

3. Sew a black-and-white print triangle to the top and bottom of the three remaining novelty print squares. Stitch a red triangle to each side of the squares.

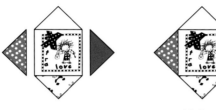

Make 3.

4. Repeat step two with the remaining red and black-and-white triangles, noting the color placement.

Make 3.

Assembling the Quilt Top

1. Refer to the quilt assembly diagram to arrange and sew the blocks into three rows of two blocks each, alternating the block color variations in each row and from row to row. Join the rows, matching seams.

2. From the leftover novelty print and black-and-white prints, cut 2½"-wide strips. Refer to "Adding Borders" on page 15 to measure the quilt top for the side borders. From the black-and-white strips, piece together two borders to the length measured. Sew the strips to the sides of the quilt top. Repeat for the top and bottom borders.

Quilt assembly

Finishing

1. Mark the quilt top with the design of your choice. Layer with batting and backing; baste. Hand or machine quilt as desired.

2. Refer to "Binding the Edges" on page 19 to cut 2¼"-wide bias strips for binding. Make a total of 146" of bias binding and sew it to the quilt.

3. Make a label and attach it to the back of the quilt.

Framed Square

By Nancy J. Martin, Kingston, Washington, 2006.
Quilted by Jacque Noard, Kingston, Washington.

Finished quilt size: 32" x 40"
Finished block size: 6" x 6"

The cheerful theme fabric is surrounded by squares in soft shades of primary colors—red, yellow, and blue. This quilt is sure to delight a little one whether your theme fabric consists of colorful dolls in native costume or rocket ships and toy trucks.

Materials

Yardages are based on 42"-wide fabrics.

1 yard of yellow striped fabric for inner border and middle pieced border

¾ yard of blue fabric for outer border and binding

½ yard of novelty print for blocks*

4 fat eighths of assorted blue fabrics for sashing and middle pieced border

3 fat eighths of assorted yellow fabrics for sashing

3 fat eighths of assorted red fabrics for sashing and middle pieced border

1¼ yards of fabric for backing

Batting and thread to finish

Additional yardage may be needed if you prefer to fussy cut the squares (see page 5).

Cutting

All measurements include ¼"-wide seam allowances.

From *each* of the 4 fat eighths of assorted blue fabrics, cut:
- 1 square, 8" x 8" (4 total)
- 6 squares, 2½" x 2½" (24 total, 3 left over)

From *each* of the 3 fat eighths of assorted red fabrics, cut:
- 1 square, 8" x 8" (3 total)
- 7 squares, 2½" x 2½" (21 total)

From *each* of the 3 fat eighths of assorted yellow fabrics, cut:
- 7 squares, 2½" x 2½" (21 total)

From the novelty print, cut:
- 6 squares, 6½" x 6½"

From the *lengthwise grain* of the yellow striped fabric, cut:
- 2 strips, 2½" x 22½"*

From the remainder of the yellow striped fabric, cut:
- 2 strips, 2½" x 26½"*
- 7 squares, 8" x 8"

From the blue fabric for outer border, cut:
- 2 strips, 3¼" x 36"
- 2 strips, 3¼" x 34"
- 1 square, 8" x 8"

Inner-border strips are cut to the exact length so the pieced middle border will fit.

Making the Rows

1. Stitch one red, one yellow, and one blue 2½" x 2½" square together. Repeat to make a total of nine vertical sashing strips, varying the fabrics and color placement in each strip.

Make 9.

2. Arrange two novelty print squares and three vertical sashing strips into a row as shown. Stitch the pieces together. Repeat to make a total of three block rows.

Make 3.

3. Stitch nine of the remaining red, yellow, and blue 2½" x 2½" squares together to make a horizontal sashing row. Repeat to make a total of four sashing rows, varying the fabrics and color placement in each row.

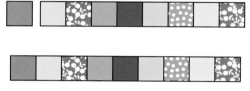

Make 4.

Assembling the Quilt Top

1. Refer to the quilt assembly diagram to join the block rows and the sashing rows, matching seams.

2. Sew the yellow striped 2½" x 26½" strips to the sides of the quilt top. Add the 2½" x 22½" strips to the top and bottom of the quilt top. These borders were cut to the exact size so that the pieced middle border would fit and should not be trimmed.

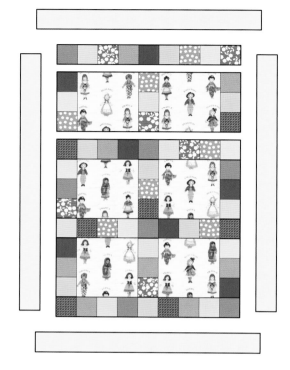

3. To make the pieced border, pair each yellow striped 8" square with a red or blue 8" square, right sides up. Referring to "Basic Bias-Square Technique" on page 10, cut and piece 2½"-wide strips, and then cut 56 bias squares, 2½" x 2½".

2½"

Cut 56.

4. Join 15 bias squares as shown to form a side border, taking care to orient the yellow striped triangles so that the stripes run toward the side of the triangle they are being sewn to. Make one additional side border with the bias squares facing the opposite direction. Refer to the quilt assembly diagram to join the borders to the sides of the quilt top, with the red and blue triangles pointing toward the quilt center.

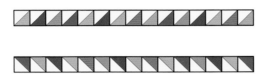

Make 1 of each.

5. Join 13 bias squares as shown to form the remaining borders. Refer to the quilt assembly diagram to sew the borders to the quilt top and bottom, taking care to position the red and blue triangles so they point toward the quilt center and noting the changes in the corners.

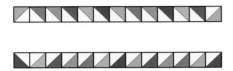

Make 1 of each.

6. Refer to "Adding Borders" on page 15 to sew the blue 3¼"-wide outer borders to the quilt top.

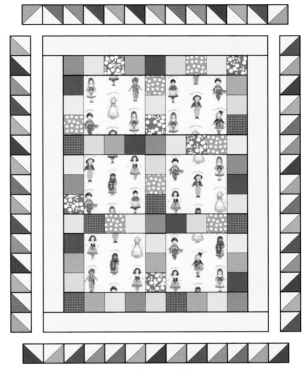

Quilt assembly

Finishing

1. Mark the quilt top with the design of your choice. Layer with batting and backing; baste. Hand or machine quilt as desired.

2. Refer to "Binding the Edges" on page 19 to cut 2¼"-wide bias strips from the remainder of the blue fabric for binding. Make a total of 154" of bias binding and sew it to the quilt.

3. Make a label and attach it to the back of the quilt.

This and That

By Nancy J. Martin, Kingston, Washington, 2006.
Quilted by Susie Hostetler, LaRue, Ohio.

Finished quilt size: 32¼" x 39"
Finished block size: 3" x 4¾"

Cheerful pigs doing this and that—skateboarding, jumping rope, and flying kites—are depicted on the novelty print that sets the theme for this quilt. When designing a quilt around novelty fabric, don't limit yourself to cuts that are square. This quilt is made from rectangles of fabric so that more of the novelty print is utilized.

Materials

Yardages are based on 42"-wide fabrics.

1 yard of novelty print for blocks and inner border*

⅓ yard of red polka-dot fabric for outer border

¼ yard *each* of 6 assorted bright red prints for blocks

¼ yard *each* of 6 assorted yellow prints for blocks

1¼ yards of fabric for backing

⅜ yard of fabric for bias binding

Batting and thread to finish

Depending on the print you select, additional yardage may be needed to fussy cut the block center rectangles (see page 5). If your print is directional, you may also need additional fabric so that the borders can be cut with all of the motifs running in the same direction.

Cutting

All measurements include ¼"-wide seam allowances. See page 5 for instructions to fussy cut the block center rectangles from the novelty fabric.

From the novelty print, fussy cut:
• 4 strips, 3¼" x 42"
• 15 rectangles, 3½" x 5¼"

From the 6 assorted bright red prints, cut a *total* of:
• 14 strips, 1½" x 42"

From the 6 assorted yellow prints, cut a *total* of:
• 10 strips, 1½" x 42"

From the red polka-dot fabric, cut:
• 4 strips, 2¼" x 42"

Making the Sashing Pieces

1. Join two bright red 1½" x 42" strips and one yellow 1½" x 42" strip as shown to make a strip set. Repeat to make a total of six strip sets. From the strip sets, cut the following pieces, varying the strip sets from which the pieces are cut so you have an assortment of fabrics in each size: 18 segments, 5¼" wide; 20 segments, 3½" wide, and 24 segments, 1½" wide.

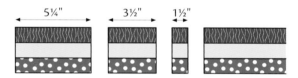

Make 6 strip sets.
Cut 18 segments, 5¼" wide.
Cut 20 segments, 3½" wide.
Cut 24 segments, 1½" wide.

2. Join two yellow 1½" x 42" strips, and one bright red 1½" x 42" strip as shown to make a strip set. Repeat to make a total of two strip sets. From the strip sets, cut 48 segments, 1½" wide.

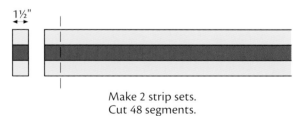

Make 2 strip sets.
Cut 48 segments.

3. Join one 1½"-wide segment from step 1 and two segments from step 2 to make a nine-patch unit. Repeat to make a total of 24 units.

Make 24.

Assembling the Quilt Top

1. Arrange and sew together four nine-patch units and three 5¼"-wide strip-set segments from step 1 of "Making the Sashing Pieces" as shown. Repeat to make a total of six sashing rows.

Make 6.

2. Arrange and sew together three novelty prints rectangles and four 3½"-wide strip-set segments as shown. Repeat to make a total of five block rows.

Make 5.

THIS AND THAT VARIATION

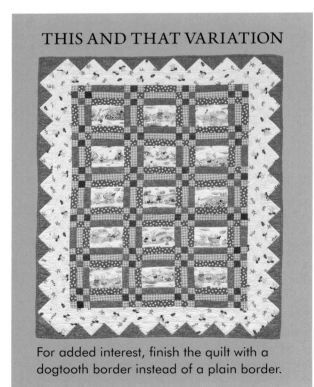

For added interest, finish the quilt with a dogtooth border instead of a plain border.

3. Refer to the quilt assembly diagram to join the block rows and the sashing rows, matching seams.

4. Refer to "Adding Borders" on page 15 to sew the 3¼"-wide inner borders to the quilt top. Repeat for the 2¼"-wide outer borders.

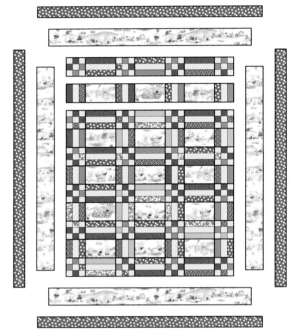

Quilt assembly

Finishing

1. Mark the quilt top with the design of your choice. Layer with batting and backing; baste. Hand or machine quilt as desired.

2. Refer to "Binding the Edges" on page 19 to cut 2¼"-wide bias strips for binding. Make a total of 152" of bias binding and sew it to the quilt.

3. Make a label and attach it to the back of the quilt.

Four-Patch Frolic

By Nancy J. Martin, Kingston, Washington, 2005.
Quilted by Jacque Noard, Kingston, Washington.

Finished quilt size: 34" x 40"
Finished block size: 3" x 3"

I love nostalgic prints from the 1930s and 1940s, and their small scale makes them an excellent choice for a baby quilt. The yellow sashing energizes the simple diagonal-set pink and green Four Patch blocks.

Materials

Yardages are based on 42"-wide fabrics.

5 fat quarters of assorted pink prints for blocks

⅞ yard of pink print for outer border and bias binding

4 fat eighths of assorted green prints for blocks

½ yard of yellow print for sashing

⅓ yard of green print for inner border

1 fat eighth of pink print for sashing squares

1¼ yards of fabric for backing

Batting and thread to finish

Cutting

All measurements include ¼"-wide seam allowances.

From *each* of the 5 fat quarters of assorted pink prints, cut:
• 2 strips, 2" x 21" (10 total)

From the remainder of the 5 fat quarters of assorted pink prints, cut a *total* of:
• 4 squares, 5½" x 5½"; cut twice diagonally to yield 16 triangles (you will have 2 left over)
• 2 squares, 3" x 3"; cut in half diagonally to yield 4 triangles

From *each* of the 4 fat eighths of assorted green prints, cut:
• 2 strips, 2" x 21" (8 total)

From the yellow print, cut:
• 80 rectangles, 1¾" x 3½"

From the pink print for sashing squares, cut:
• 31 squares, 1¾" x 1¾"
• 5 squares, 2½" x 2½"; cut twice diagonally to yield 20 triangles (you will have 2 left over)

From the green print for inner border, cut:
• 4 strips, 2" x 42"

From the pink print for outer border, cut:
• 4 strips, 3¾" x 42"

Making the Blocks

1. Join two pink 2" x 21" strips to make a strip set. Repeat to make a total of five strip sets. From the strip sets, cut 40 segments, 2" wide.

Make 5 strip sets.
Cut 40 segments.

2. Stitch two different segments together to make a Four Patch block. Repeat to make a total of 20 pink Four Patch blocks.

Make 20.

3. Join two green 2" x 21" strips to make a strip set. Repeat to make a total of four strip sets. From the strip sets, cut 24 segments, 2" wide.

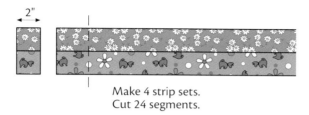

Make 4 strip sets.
Cut 24 segments.

4. Stitch two different segments together to make a Four Patch block. Repeat to make a total of 12 green Four Patch blocks.

Make 12.

Assembling the Quilt Top

1. Arrange the pink and green Four Patch blocks, the yellow 1¾" x 3½" sashing rectangles, the pink 1¾" sashing squares, and the large and small pink setting triangles into diagonal rows. Sew the pieces in each row together, and then sew the rows together, matching seams. Add the corner setting triangles last.

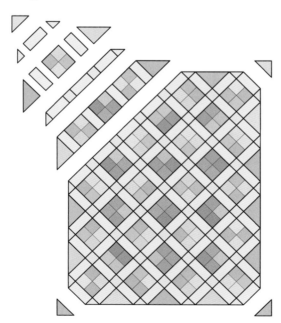

2. Refer to "Adding Borders" on page 15 to sew the green 2"-wide inner borders to the quilt top. Repeat for the pink 3¾"-wide outer borders.

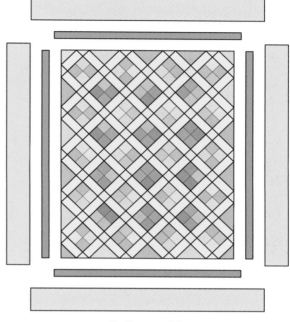

Quilt assembly

Finishing

1. Mark the quilt top with the design of your choice. Layer with batting and backing; baste. Hand or machine quilt as desired.

2. Refer to "Binding the Edges" on page 19 to cut 2¼"-wide bias strips for binding. Make a total of 158" of bias binding and sew it to the quilt.

3. Make a label and attach it to the back of the quilt.

Nana's First Quilt

By Nancy J. Martin, Kingston, Washington, 2006.
Quilted by Frankie Schmitt, Kenmore, Washington.

Finished quilt size: 32½" x 44½"
Finished block size: 12" x 12"

The arrival of the first grandbaby, or a new grandchild, is often an enticement to get women quilting. Here is the perfect quilt for the beginning quilter, one that will be appreciated by the new arrival.

Materials

Yardages are based on 42"-wide fabrics.

9 fat eighths of assorted small-scale blue plaids for blocks and outer border

⅞ yard of light blue fabric for blocks, inner border, and binding

1⅛ yards of large-scale blue plaid

1⅜ yards of fabric for backing

Batting and thread to finish

Cutting

All measurements include ¼"-wide seam allowances.

From *each* of the 9 fat eighths of assorted small-scale blue plaids, cut:

• 14 squares, 2½" x 2½" (126 total)

From the light blue fabric, cut:

• 6 squares, 7¼" x 7¼"; cut twice diagonally to yield 24 triangles

• 2 strips, 2½" x 36½"*

• 2 strips, 2½" x 28½"*

From the large-scale blue plaid, cut:

• 12 squares, 6⅞" x 6⅞"; cut in half diagonally to yield 24 triangles

*Inner-border strips are cut to the exact length so that the pieced outer border will fit.

Making the Blocks

1. Stitch nine of the assorted blue plaid squares together to make a nine-patch unit. Repeat to make a total of six units.

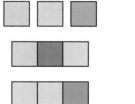

Make 6.

2. Stitch a light blue triangle to each side of the nine-patch units, stitching opposite sides first.

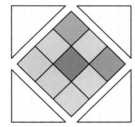 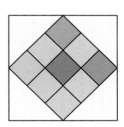

Make 6.

3. Stitch a large-scale blue plaid triangle to each side of the units from step 2, stitching opposite sides first.

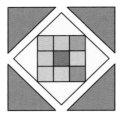

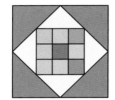

Make 6.

Assembling the Quilt Top

1. Stitch two blocks together to make a row. Repeat to make a total of three rows.

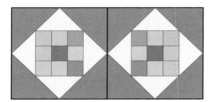

Make 3.

2. Refer to the quilt assembly diagram to stitch the rows together, matching seams.

3. Sew the light blue 2½" x 36½" border strips to the sides of the quilt top. Sew the light blue 2½" x 28½" border strips to the top and bottom of the quilt top. These borders were cut to the exact size so that the pieced outer border would fit and should not be trimmed.

4. Stitch 20 assorted blue plaid squares together end to end to make a side border. Repeat to make one additional border. Join the borders to the sides of the quilt top.

5. Stitch 16 assorted blue plaid squares together end to end to make the top border. Repeat to make the bottom border. Join the borders to the top and bottom of the quilt top.

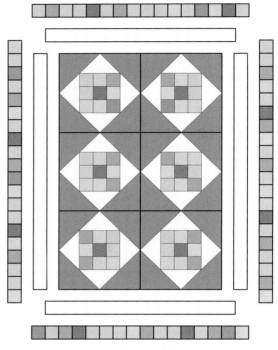

Quilt assembly

Finishing

1. Mark the quilt top with the design of your choice. Layer with batting and backing; baste. Hand or machine quilt as desired.

2. Refer to "Binding the Edges" on page 19 to cut 2¼"-wide bias strips from the remaining light blue fabric. Make a total of 162" of bias binding and sew it to the quilt.

3. Make a label and attach it to the back of the quilt.

Baby Sukey

By Nancy J. Martin, Kingston, Washington, 2006.
Quilted by Suzie Hostetler, LaRue, Ohio.

Finished quilt size: 30½" x 44½"
Finished block size: 12" x 12"

Baby Sukey is a variation of one of my favorite blocks, "Aunt Sukey's Choice." Each block's center square features '30s reproduction fabric, depicting the "Little Boy Blue" nursery rhyme. Additional reproduction prints in soft greens and rose make this a charming quilt for either a boy or girl.

Materials

Yardages are based on 42"-wide fabrics.

6 fat quarters of assorted light green prints for blocks and sashing

6 fat eighths of assorted green reproduction prints for blocks and sashing

6 fat eighths of assorted rose fabrics for blocks

1 fat quarter of green novelty print for block centers

⅜ yard of rose fabric for bias binding

1½ yards of fabric for backing

Batting and thread to finish

Cutting

All measurements include ¼"-wide seam allowances.

From *each* of the 6 fat quarters of assorted light green prints, cut:
• 2 squares, 8" x 8" (12 total)
• 8 squares, 2½" x 2½" (48 total)
• 3 rectangles, 2½" x 12½" (18 total; you will have 1 left over)

From *each* of the 6 fat eighths of assorted rose fabrics, cut:
• 2 squares, 8" x 8" (12 total)

From the fat quarter of green novelty print, cut:
• 6 squares, 4½" x 4½"

From *each* of the 6 fat eighths of assorted green reproduction prints, cut:
• 10 squares, 2½" x 2½" (60 total)

Making the Blocks

1. Pair each assorted light green 8" square with an assorted rose 8" square, right sides up. Referring to "Basic Bias-Square Technique" on page 10, cut and piece 2½"-wide strips, and then cut 96 bias squares, 2½" x 2½".

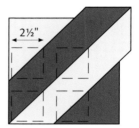

Cut 96.

2. Join the light green sides of two bias squares together. Repeat to make a total of 24 bias-square units.

Make 24.

3. Stitch a bias-square unit to the top and bottom of a novelty print 4½" square.

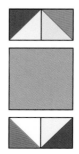 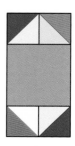

Make 6.

4. Join a green reproduction print 2½" square to each end of the remaining bias-square units. Join these units to the sides of each unit made in step 3.

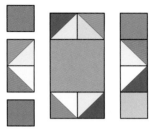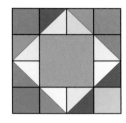

Make 6.

5. Join the rose sides of two of the remaining bias squares together. Repeat to make a total of 24 bias-square units.

Make 24.

6. Stitch a light green 2½" square to each end of the bias-square units. Join one of these units to the top and bottom of each unit from step 4.

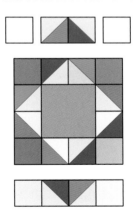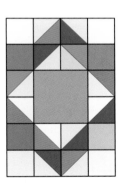

Make 6.

7. Add a light green 2½" square and a green reproduction print 2½" square to each end of the 12 remaining bias-square units from step 6. Stitch these units to the sides of each unit from step 6 to complete the blocks.

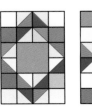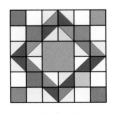

Make 6.

Assembling the Quilt Top

1. Join two blocks and three light green 2½" x 12½" sashing strips to make a block row. Make three block rows.

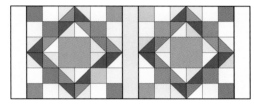

Make 3.

2. Join two light green 2½" x 12½" sashing strips and three green reproduction print 2½" squares to make a sashing row. Make four sashing rows.

Make 4.

3. Refer to the quilt assembly diagram to join the block rows and the sashing rows, matching seams.

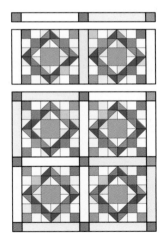

Quilt assembly

Finishing

1. Mark the quilt top with the design of your choice. Layer with batting and backing; baste. Hand or machine quilt as desired.

2. Refer to "Binding the Edges" on page 19 to cut 2¼"-wide bias strips for binding. Make a total of 158" of bias binding and sew it to the quilt.

3. Make a label and attach it to the back of the quilt.

Into the Woods

By Nancy J. Martin, Kingston, Washington, 2006.
Quilted by Suzie Hostetler, LaRue, Ohio.

Finished quilt size: 33" x 43"
Finished block size: 9" x 9"

The Wild West theme abounds in this quilt for a baby boy. Change the novelty print fabric in the center square to something soft and feminine, and you'll have the perfect "girly-girl" quilt.

Materials

Yardages are based on 42"-wide fabrics.

1 yard of light green novelty print for block centers, outer border, and binding

⅔ yard of tan print for blocks and sashing

⅝ yard of yellow striped fabric for blocks

½ yard of rust print for blocks

½ yard of light green striped fabric for blocks and inner border

1 fat eighth of turquoise fabric for blocks

1⅜ yard of fabric for backing

Batting and thread to finish

Cutting

All measurements include ¼"-wide seam allowances.

From the yellow striped fabric, cut:
• 6 squares, 7" x 7"
• 6 squares, 4¼" x 4¼"; cut twice diagonally to yield 24 triangles
• 24 squares, 2" x 2"

From the rust print, cut:
• 6 squares, 7" x 7"

From the turquoise fabric, cut:
• 24 squares, 2" x 2"

From the light green striped fabric, cut:
• 4 strips, 2½" x 42"
• 6 squares, 4¼" x 4¼"; cut twice diagonally to yield 24 triangles

From the tan print, cut:
• 4 strips, 2" x 23"
• 9 strips, 2" x 9½"
• 12 squares, 4¼" x 4¼"; cut twice diagonally to yield 48 triangles

From the light green novelty print, cut:
• 2 strips, 3¼" x 39"
• 2 strips, 3¼" x 34"
• 6 squares, 3½" x 3½"

Making the Blocks

1. Pair each yellow 7" square with a rust 7" square, right sides up. Referring to "Basic Bias-Square Technique" on page 10, cut and piece 2"-wide strips, and then cut 48 bias squares, 2" x 2".

Cut 48.

2. Make 24 of unit 1 using two bias squares, one turquoise 2" square, and one yellow 2" square.

Unit 1.
Cut 24.

3. Make 24 of unit 2 using two tan triangles, one yellow triangle, and one light green striped triangle.

Unit 2.
Cut 24.

4. Join two of unit 1 to a unit 2 to make a row. Repeat to make a total of 12 top/bottom rows.

Make 12.

5. Join two of unit 2 to the sides of a novelty print 3½" square to make a center row. Repeat to make a total of six rows.

Make 6.

6. Join the rows as shown to make six blocks.

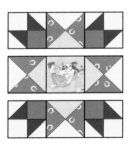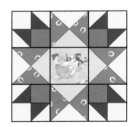

Make 6.

Assembling the Quilt Top

1. Join two blocks and three tan 2" x 9½" strips to make a row. Repeat to make a total of three block rows.

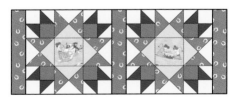

Make 3.

2. Refer to the quilt assembly diagram to join the block rows and the tan 2" x 23" strips, matching seams.

3. Refer to "Adding Borders" on page 15 to sew the light green striped 2½"-wide inner borders to the quilt top. Repeat to add the novelty print 3¼"-wide outer borders.

Quilt assembly

Finishing

1. Mark the quilt top with the design of your choice. Layer with batting and backing; baste. Hand or machine quilt as desired.

2. Refer to "Binding the Edges" on page 19 to cut 2¼"-wide bias strips from the remainder of the novelty print for binding. Make a total of 160" of bias binding and sew it to the quilt.

3. Make a label and attach it to the back of the quilt.

Broken Star

By Nancy J. Martin, Kingston, Washington, 2005.
Quilted by Sarah Borntrager, Kenton, Ohio.

Finished quilt size: 30" x 37½"
Finished block size: 6" x 6"

Dig into your scrap bag to find little bits of bright and cheery prints for this charming quilt. The blue used for the various star tips is similar in color to the energizing blue polka-dot border fabric.

Materials

Yardages are based on 42"-wide fabrics.

10 fat eighths of assorted blue fabrics for blocks and sashing squares

8 fat eighths of assorted yellow, green, pink, blue, and violet fabrics for blocks and sashing squares

8 fat eighths of assorted light background fabrics for blocks

6 fat eighths of assorted light blue fabrics for blocks

½ yard of cream print for sashing

⅝ yard of blue print for border and binding

Batting and thread to finish

Cutting

All measurements include ¼"-wide seam allowances.

From *each* of the 10 fat eighths of assorted blue fabrics, cut:
• 5 squares, 2⅜" x 2⅜"; cut in half diagonally to yield 10 triangles (100 total; you will have 4 left over)
• 1 square, 2" x 2" (10 total)

From *each* of the 6 fat eighths of assorted light blue fabrics, cut:
• 2 squares, 4¼" x 4¼"; cut twice diagonally to yield 8 triangles (48 total)

From *each* of the 8 fat eighths of assorted yellow, green, pink, blue, and violet fabrics, cut:
• 2 squares, 7" x 7" (16 total)
• 1 square, 2" x 2"; cut an extra square from 2 of the fabrics (10 total)

From *each* of the 8 fat eighths of assorted light background fabrics, cut:
• 2 squares, 7" x 7" (16 total)

From the cream print, cut:
• 31 strips, 2" x 6½"

From the blue print, cut:
• 4 strips, 3¼" x 42"

Making the Blocks

1. Join two blue triangles to a light blue triangle. Repeat to make a total of 48 flying-geese units.

Make 48.

2. Pair a light background 7" square with each yellow, green, pink, blue, and violet 7" square, right sides up. Referring to "Basic Bias-Square Technique" on page 10, cut and piece 2"-wide strips, and then cut 96 bias squares, 2" x 2".

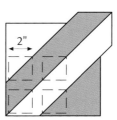

Cut 96.

3. Stitch four bias squares together to make the block center. Add a flying-geese unit to the sides of the center unit. Repeat to make a total of 12 center rows.

Make 12.

4. Stitch a bias square to the ends of one of the remaining flying-geese units to make a top/bottom row. Repeat to make a total of 24 rows.

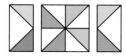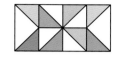

Make 24.

5. Join the rows as shown to make 12 blocks.

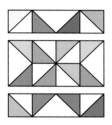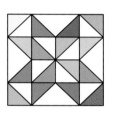

Make 12.

Assembling the Quilt Top

1. Join three blocks and four cream sashing strips to make a block row. Repeat to make a total of four rows.

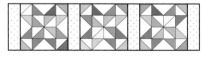

Make 4.

2. Join four 2" squares and three sashing strips to make a sashing row. Repeat to make a total of five rows.

Make 5.

3. Refer to the quilt assembly diagram to join the block rows and the sashing rows, matching seams.

4. Refer to "Adding Borders" on page 15 to sew the blue 3¼"-wide borders to the quilt top.

Quilt assembly

Finishing

1. Mark the quilt top with the design of your choice. Layer with batting and backing; baste. Hand or machine quilt as desired.

2. Refer to "Binding the Edges" on page 19 to cut 2¼"-wide bias strips from the remainder of the blue print for binding. Make a total of 145" of bias binding and sew it to the quilt.

3. Make a label and attach it to the back of the quilt.

Baby's First Christmas

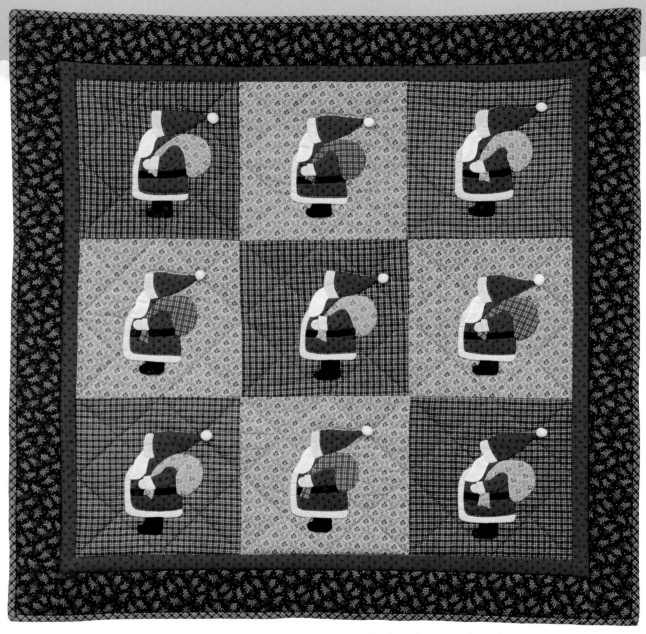

By Nancy J. Martin, Kingston, Washington, 2007.
Quilted by Freda Smith, Bothell, Washington.

Finished quilt size: 35" x 35"
Finished block size: 9" x 9"

This shy Santa reminds me of Sunbonnet Sue, who also has a round tummy and hides her face. Santa's sack is full of presents for a baby's first Christmas. Whether used as a wall hanging or in the crib, this quilt is sure to bring Christmas joy.

Materials

Yardages are based on 42"-wide fabrics.

¾ yard of green plaid for block backgrounds and bias binding

½ yard of dark green print for outer border

⅜ yard of light green print for block backgrounds

¼ yard of red print for inner border

¼ yard of red print for coats and hats

1 fat eighth or scrap of black fabric for belts and boots

1 fat eighth or scrap of light print for hat and coat trim

1 fat eighth or scrap of white print for beards

1 fat eighth or scrap of pink fabric for hands

⅛ yard *total* of red plaid and red print for Santa's sacks

1¼ yards of fabric for backing

Batting and thread to finish

Cardboard or template plastic

Bond-weight paper or freezer paper

9 white pom-poms for hats (approximately ¼"-diameter each)*

* Pom-poms can be a choking hazard for babies and small children. Consider replacing the pom-poms with appliquéd circles if the quilt will not be used as a wall hanging.

Cutting

All measurements include ¼"-wide seam allowances.

From the green plaid, cut:
• 5 squares, 10" x 10"

From the light green print, cut:
• 4 squares, 10" x 10"

From the red print for the inner border, cut:
• 4 strips, 1½" x 42"

From the dark green print, cut:
• 4 strips, 3¼" x 42"

Making the Blocks

1. Using the cardboard or template plastic, make a template of each shape in the appliqué design on page 53. Don't add seam allowances to the templates.

2. On bond-weight paper or freezer paper, trace around the templates to make a paper patch for each shape in the appliqué.

3. Pin or iron each paper patch to the wrong side of the appropriate fabric. If using freezer paper, pin with the plastic-coated side facing up.

4. Cut out the fabric shapes, adding a ⅛"-wide seam allowance around each paper shape.

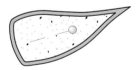

5. With your fingers, turn the seam allowance over the edge of the paper and baste to the paper. Clip corners and do inside curves first. (A little clipping may be necessary to help the fabric stretch.) On outside curves, take small running stitches through the fabric only, to ease in fullness.

6. When all the seam allowances are turned and basted, press the appliqué pieces.

7. Fold the background squares into quarters and lightly crease the folds to mark the center.

8. Position and pin the appliqué pieces in place on the background squares, working in numerical order.

9. Use a small blind hem stitch and a single strand of thread that matches the appliqué (for example, red thread for the coats) to appliqué shapes to the background squares. Start the first stitch from the back of the block. Bring the needle up through the background fabric and through the folded edge of the appliqué piece. Insert the needle right next to where you brought it up, but this time put it through only the background fabric. Bring the needle up through the background fabric and then into the appliqué piece, approximately ⅛" or less from the first stitch. Space your stitches a little less than ⅛" apart.

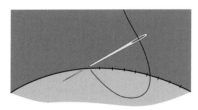

10. When the appliqué is complete, slit the background fabric behind the appliqué shape and pull out the paper patches. Press the appliqué, and then trim all of the blocks to 9½" x 9½".

Make 5.

Make 4.

Assembling the Quilt Top

1. Refer to the quilt assembly diagram to arrange and sew the blocks into three rows of three blocks each, alternating the plaid and print background blocks in each row and from row to row. Join the rows, matching seams.

2. Refer to "Adding Borders" on page 15 to sew the red 1½"-wide inner borders to the quilt top. Repeat to add the green print 3¼"-wide outer borders.

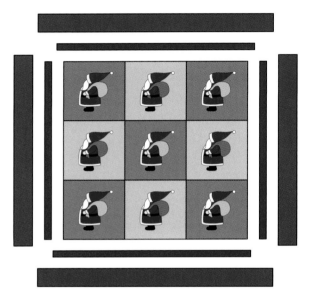
Quilt assembly

Finishing

1. Mark the quilt top with the design of your choice. Layer with batting and backing; baste. Hand or machine quilt as desired.

2. Refer to "Binding the Edges" on page 19 to cut 2¼"-wide bias strips from the remainder of the green plaid fabric for binding. Make a total of 150" of bias binding and sew it to the quilt.

3. Tack a pom-pom to the tip of each hat.

4. Make a label and attach it to the back of the quilt.

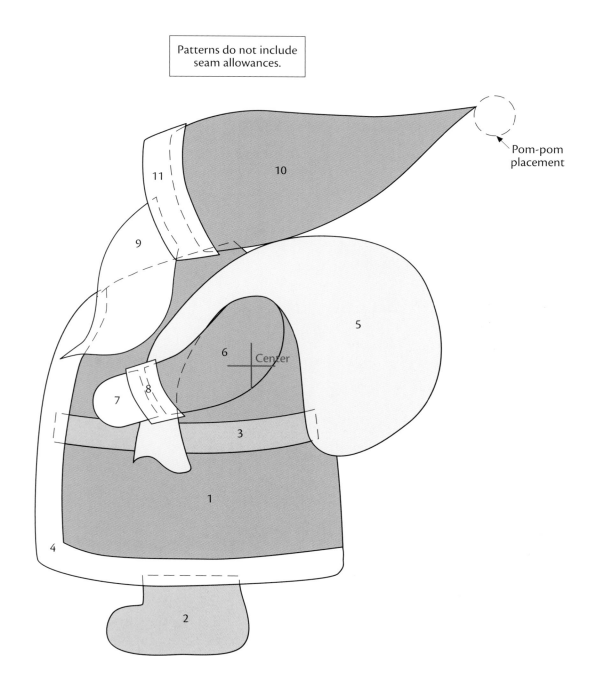

Patterns do not include seam allowances.

Pom-pom placement

10

11

9

5

6 | Center

7

8

3

1

4

2

Paper Dolls

By Nancy J. Martin, Kingston, Washington, 2008.
Quilted by Shelly Nolte, Kingston, Washington.

Finished quilt size: 29" x 41"
Finished block size: 8" x 8"

couldn't resist this novelty print that reminded me of the paper dolls I played with in my childhood. The paper dolls are showcased in the star centers and enlivened by the cheery yellow-and-blue color scheme.

Materials

Yardages are based on 42"-wide fabrics.

⅔ yard of novelty print for block centers and outer border*

5 fat eighths of assorted blue prints for blocks and sashing

5 fat eighths of assorted yellow prints for blocks and sashing

¼ yard or 1 fat quarter of blue print for sashing squares

¼ yard of blue fabric for inner border

⅜ yard of fabric for bias binding

1½ yards of fabric for backing

Batting and thread to finish

Additional yardage may be needed if you prefer to fussy cut the squares and outer border (see page 5). If your print is directional, you may also need additional fabric so that the borders can be cut with all of the motifs running in the same direction.

Cutting

All measurements include ¼"-wide seam allowances.

From *each* of the 5 fat eighths of assorted blue prints, cut:

• 8 squares, 2⅞" x 2⅞"; cut in half diagonally to yield 16 triangles (80 total; you will have 4 left over)

From *each* of the 5 fat eighths of assorted yellow prints, cut:

• 2 squares, 5¼" x 5¼"; cut twice diagonally to yield 8 triangles (40 total; you will have 2 left over)
• 24 squares, 2½" x 2½"

From the novelty print, cut:
• 8 squares, 4½" x 4½"
• 4 strips, 3¾" x 42"

From the blue print for sashing squares, cut:
• 7 squares, 4½" x 4½"

From the blue fabric for inner border, cut:
• 4 strips, 1½" x 42"

Making the Blocks and Sashing Units

1. Join two assorted blue triangles to a yellow triangle to make a triangle unit. Repeat to make a total of 38 units.

Make 38.

2. Arrange and sew together four triangle units, four yellow 2½" squares, and one novelty print 4½" square to make a block. Repeat to make a total of six blocks.

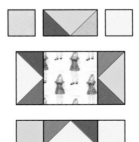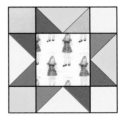

Make 6.

3. Join two triangle units to a blue print 4½" square to make a sashing unit. Repeat to make a total of seven units.

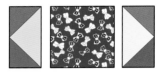

Make 7.

Assembling the Quilt Top

1. Join two blocks and one sashing unit to make a block row. Repeat to make a total of three rows.

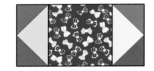

Make 3.

2. Join two sashing units and one novelty print square to make a sashing row. Repeat to make a total of two rows.

Make 2.

3. Sew the sashing rows between the block rows, matching seams.

4. Refer to "Adding Borders" on page 15 to sew the blue 1½"-wide inner borders to the quilt top. Repeat with the novelty print 3¾"-wide outer borders.

Quilt assembly

Finishing

1. Mark the quilt top with the design of your choice. Layer with batting and backing; baste. Hand or machine quilt as desired.

2. Refer to "Binding the Edges" on page 19 to cut 2¼"-wide bias strips for binding. Make a total of 150" of bias binding and sew it to the quilt.

3. Make a label and attach it to the back of the quilt.

Beach Balls

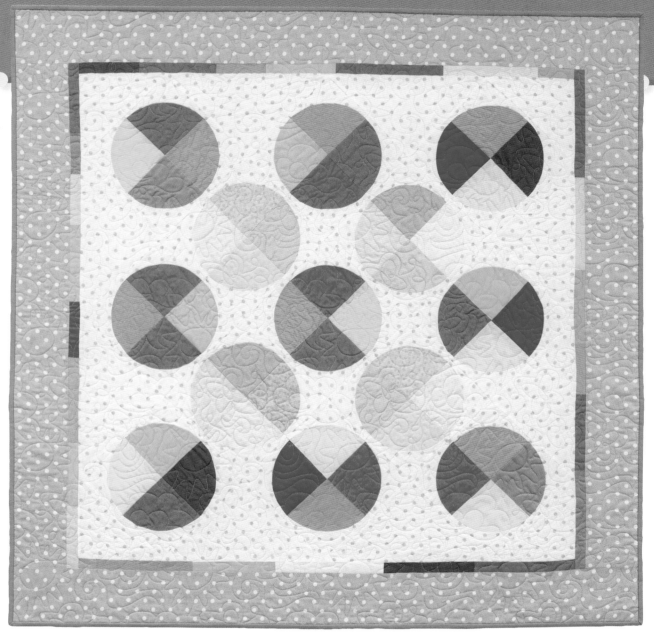

By Cleo Nollette, Seattle, Washington, 2008.

Quilted by Shelly Nolte, Kingston, Washington.

Finished quilt size: 45½" x 45½"

Finished block size: 8½" x 8½"

*B*each Balls will brighten up a seaside nursery with a profusion of cheerful colors. The easy curved-seam piecing makes this colorful quilt a snap to stitch in a jiffy. Any baby would be happy to watch these bouncing beach balls.

Materials

Yardages are based on 42"-wide fabrics.

11 fat quarters of assorted bright solid and tone-on-tone fabrics for blocks and inner border

1½ yards of polka-dot fabric for outer border

1⅓ yards of polka-dot fabric for background

⅜ yard of fabric for bias binding

3 yards of fabric for backing

Batting and thread to finish

Template plastic

Cutting

All measurements include ¼"-wide seam allowances. Templates are on page 60.

From *each* of the 11 fat quarters, cut:
• 5 template A pieces (55 total; you will have 3 left over)
• 1 strip, 1¼" x 16" (11 total)

From the polka-dot fabric for background, cut:
• 4 strips, 7" x 42"; crosscut into:
  • 26 rectangles, 5" x 7"
  • 2 squares, 7" x 7"; cut in half diagonally to yield 4 corner setting triangles
• 2 squares, 13½" x 13½"; cut twice diagonally to yield 8 side setting triangles

From the *lengthwise grain* of the polka-dot fabric for outer border, cut:
• 2 strips, 4¼" x 38"
• 2 strips, 4¼" x 45½"

Making the Blocks

1. Cut two template B pieces from each polka-dot background rectangle.

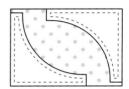

2. Fold the template A and B pieces in half along the curved edges to mark the centers; finger-press the fold at the curved edges. Clip into the seam allowance along the curved edge of each B piece.

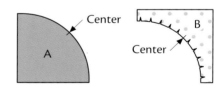

3. Place a B piece on top of an A piece, matching one outer edge and the centers. Pin in place, and then slowly stitch from the outer edge to the center mark, stopping with the needle down.

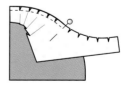

4. Move the pin to the opposite outer edge and continue sewing slowly until you reach the end.

5. Repeat steps 3 and 4 to make a total of 52 units. Press the seam allowances from the front of the piece, pressing toward the template A pieces.

Make 52.

6. Randomly join four units to make a Beach Ball block. Repeat to make a total of 13 blocks.

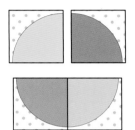

Make 13.

Assembling the Quilt Top

1. Arrange the Beach Ball blocks and the polka-dot side setting triangles into diagonal rows. Sew the pieces in each row together, and then sew the rows together, matching seams. Add the corner setting triangles last.

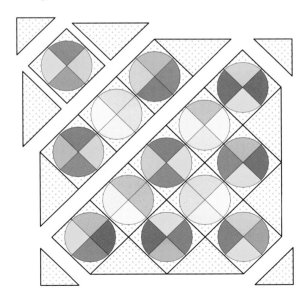

2. Stitch the 1¼" x 16" strips together end to end in random order to make one long strip.

3. Refer to "Adding Borders" on page 15 to cut the pieced strip to the required lengths and sew them to the quilt top for the inner border. Repeat for the polka dot 4¼"-wide outer borders.

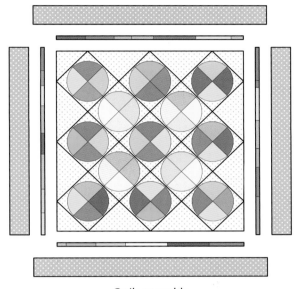

Quilt assembly

Finishing

1. Mark the quilt top with the design of your choice. Layer with batting and backing; baste. Hand or machine quilt as desired.

2. Refer to "Binding the Edges" on page 19 to cut 2¼"- wide bias strips for binding. Make a total of 195" of bias binding and sew it to the quilt.

3. Make a label and attach it to the back of the quilt.

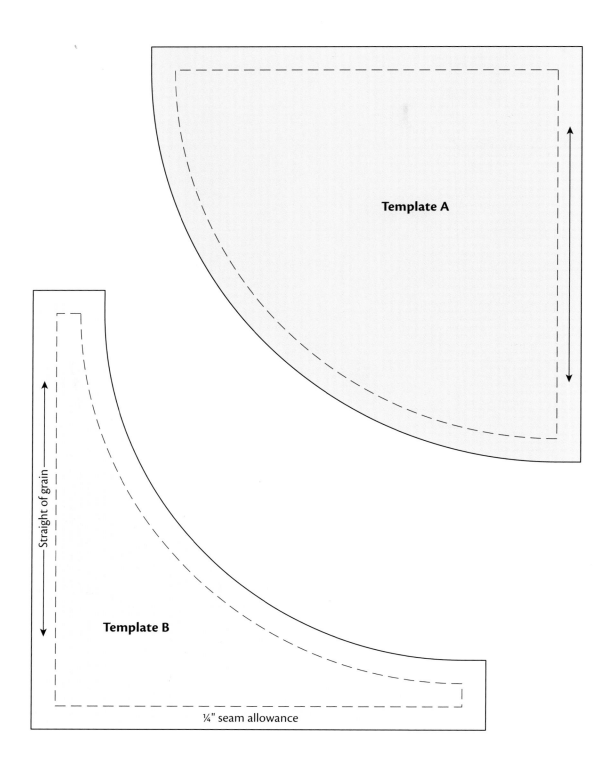

Template A

Straight of grain

Template B

¼" seam allowance

Big Boy Blue

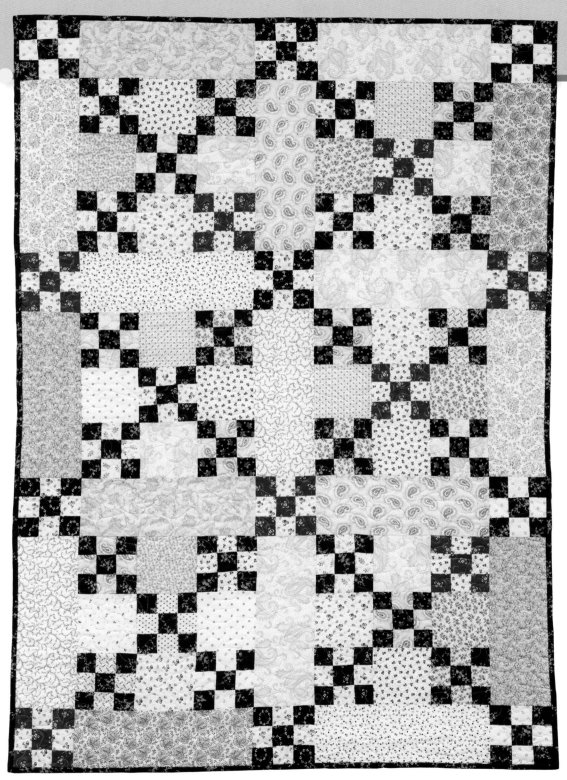

By Nancy J. Martin, Kingston, Washington, 2008.
Quilted by Shelly Nolte, Kingston, Washington.

Finished quilt size: 34¼" x 49¼"
Finished block size: 11¼" x 11¼"

$\mathcal{B}$ig Boy Blue is a traditional quilt, with its treasured Double Nine Patch design and classic blue-and-white color scheme. This quilt's name makes me picture grandmas everywhere asking their little grandsons "Who's my big boy?"

Materials

Yardages are based on 42"-wide fabrics.

8 fat quarters of assorted light prints for blocks and sashing

8 fat quarters of assorted blue prints for blocks and sashing

⅜ yard of fabric for bias binding

1⅝ yards of fabric for backing

Batting and thread to finish

Cutting

All measurements include ¼"-wide seam allowances.

From *each* of the 8 fat quarters of assorted blue prints, cut:

• 2 strips, 1¾" x 21" (16 total)
• 1 strip, 1¾" x 10½" (8 total)

From *each* of the 8 fat quarters of assorted light prints, cut:

• 2 strips, 1¾" x 21" (16 total)
• 2 strips, 4¼" x 11¾". Cut one additional strip from one fat quarter (17 total).
• 3 squares, 4¼" x 4¼" (24 total)

Making the Nine-Patch Units and Blocks

1. Using the 1¾" x 21" strips, stitch two matching blue strips and one light strip together to make strip set A. Repeat to make a total of eight strip sets. From *each* strip set, cut 10 segments, 1¾" wide. From *two* of the strip sets, cut two additional segments (84 total).

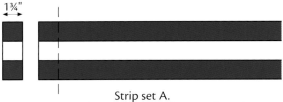

1¾"

Strip set A.
Make 8. Cut 10 segments from each and 2 additional segments from two (84 total).

2. Cut the remaining light 1¾" x 21" strips in half lengthwise. Using the same fabric combinations you used for the A strip sets, sew the light half strips and the blue 1¾" x 10½" strips together to make strip set B. From *each* strip set, cut five segments. Cut *one* additional segment from each of the two fabric combinations from which you cut the additional A segments (42 total).

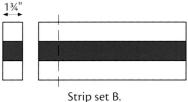

1¾"

Strip set B.
Make 8. Cut 5 segments from each and 2 additional segments from two (42 total).

3. Using segments with the same fabric combinations, join two A segments and one B segment to make a nine-patch unit. Repeat to make a total of 42 nine-patch units.

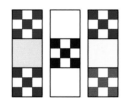

Make 42.

4. Stitch five nine-patch units and four light 4¼" squares together to make a Double Nine Patch block. Repeat to make a total of six blocks.

Make 6.

Assembling the Quilt Top

1. Join two blocks and three light 4¼" x 11¾" strips to make a block row. Repeat to make a total of three rows.

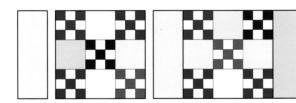

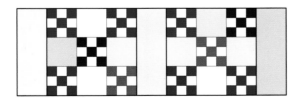

Make 3.

2. Join three of the remaining nine-patch units and two light 4¼" x 11¾" strips to make a sashing row. Repeat to make a total of four rows.

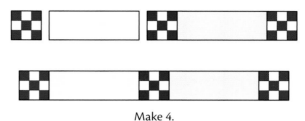

Make 4.

3. Join the block rows and the sashing rows, matching seams.

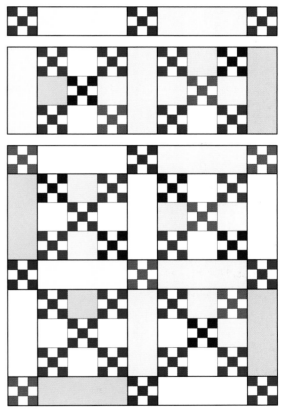

Quilt assembly

Finishing

1. Mark the quilt top with the design of your choice. Layer with batting and backing; baste. Hand or machine quilt as desired.

2. Refer to "Binding the Edges" on page 19 to cut 2¼"-wide bias strips for binding. Make a total of 177" of bias binding and sew it to the quilt.

3. Make a label and attach it to the back of the quilt.

About the Author

Nancy J. Martin is a talented teacher and quiltmaker who has written more than 40 books on quiltmaking. An innovator in the quilting industry, she introduced the Bias Square® cutting ruler to quilters everywhere.

Along with having more than 25 years of teaching experience and several best-selling titles to her credit, Nancy is the founder of Martingale & Company, the publisher of America's Best-Loved Quilt Books. She and her husband, Dan, enjoy living in the Pacific Northwest.